D1643592

BRITAIN
AND THE TIDE OF
WORLD AFFAIRS

BRITAIN
AND THE TIDE OF
WORLD AFFAIRS

by

OLIVER S. FRANKS

The B.B.C. Reith Lectures
1954

GEOFFREY CUMBERLEGE
OXFORD UNIVERSITY PRESS
LONDON
1955

BRITAIN
AND THE TIDE OF
WORLD AFFAIRS

By

OLIVER S. FRANKS

The B.B.C. Reith Lectures
1954

GEOFFREY CUMBERLEGE
OXFORD UNIVERSITY PRESS
LONDON
1955

Oxford University Press, Amen House, London, E.C.4

GLASGOW   NEW YORK   TORONTO   MELBOURNE   WELLINGTON
BOMBAY   CALCUTTA   MADRAS   KARACHI   CAPE TOWN   IBADAN

Geoffrey Cumberlege, Publisher to the University

FOREWORD

THIS book contains the Reith Lectures for 1954. They are printed as they were given, almost without change; discourses written to be listened to.

I hope my readers will forgive this and at the same time will find what I have said about Britain's position and policies in the world sufficiently simple, clear and positive to make them ask themselves whether they agree or disagree. I hope too that, if they disagree, they will go on enquiring until they have reached better results. For I am sure that Britain can be a leader among the nations in the future as she has been in the past. But whether this will happen is not certain. It depends first on the thoroughness with which we think through the effect on our country of the great changes in the world, and secondly on the effort we make to find and apply broad policies which are appropriate to this changed world in which we have to live.

I should like to express my gratitude to Mr. G. R. Lewin of the B.B.C. for the skill and patience with which he taught me some of the rules for writing the spoken word.

1955   O.S.F.

CONTENTS

CONTENTS

I

BRITAIN IN A CHANGED WORLD

THESE lectures give me a chance to talk about some opinions which have formed themselves in my mind about Britain and her future, opinions that have come to me mainly as a result of my tour of duty as British Ambassador in Washington. I was there for four-and-a-half years, half the time since the end of the second world war. I was in continuous contact with the American Administration and the American people, as I explained and advocated British policies and actions. In return, American views and feelings were continuously impressed upon me. This life of incessant discussion and argument made me think afresh about a great many things, in particular, it caused me to reflect on Britain. I encountered such a variety of views on where the tide of world affairs was taking us. Some of the judgements were pessimistic, some were optimistic, most were friendly, but nearly all were different from my own assumptions. I was forced to try to think out my own position more clearly. And I have gone on with this attempt since I came home and resumed my ordinary life.

This is the origin of the opinions I want to put before you. They claim no authority; they express no official view, but I believe them to be true and their subject is important. I should like to persuade you of their truth and urgency. If I do not have the good fortune to win your agreement, I hope at least to convince you that the issues are real. I should like you to feel that, if the answers I suggest will not do, you will not be content until you have found better ones.

I believe that history has given us a period within which to work out our problems. The period began with the end of the second world war and may last as long as the working lifetime of my generation. It will not be longer; it may

I

BRITAIN IN A CHANGED WORLD

THESE lectures give me a chance to talk about some opinions which have formed themselves in my mind about Britain and her future, opinions that have come to me mainly as a result of my tour of duty as British Ambassador in Washington. I was there for four-and-a-half years, half the time since the end of the second world war. I was in continuous contact with the American Administration and the American people, as I explained and advocated British policies and actions. In return, American views and feelings were continuously impressed upon me. This life of incessant discussion and argument made me think afresh about a great many things: in particular, it caused me to reflect on Britain. I encountered such a variety of views on where the tide of world affairs was taking us. Some of the judgements were pessimistic, some were optimistic, most were friendly, but nearly all were different from my own assumptions. I was forced to try to think out my own position more clearly. And I have gone on with this attempt since I came home and resumed my ordinary life.

This is the origin of the opinions I want to put before you. They claim no authority: they express no official view. But I believe them to be true and their subject is important. I should like to persuade you of their truth and urgency. If I do not have the good fortune to win your agreement, I hope at least to convince you that the issues are real. I should like you to feel that, if the answers I suggest will not do, you will not be content until you have found better ones.

I believe that history has given us a period within which to work out our problems. The period began with the end of the second world war and may last as long as the working lifetime of my generation. It will not be longer: it may well be shorter. Within the period no one year or the decisions made in it are likely to be in the strict sense crucial, neither this year, nor next year, nor the year after. Within the period there is always still time. But the whole period, whatever its duration may turn out to be, is crucial: what we do or fail to do in it will be decisive. After it there will be no second chance.

I propose in these lectures to try to make a positive contribution, the beginning of an answer to the problems as I see them. I shall set myself to describe, so far as I can, some of the conditions in the world of which we have to take account if Britain is to stay great, and, given these conditions, what are some of the means we must adopt to achieve and maintain our purpose.

There are some who suggest that the future of Britain lies in making a break with the past and giving up the traditions of greatness. The thing to do is to withdraw from world affairs and lead a quiet life on our island, democratic, contented and reasonably industrious. This is impossible. Geography and history alike forbid it. For us there is no middle way. Nor do most of us really think there is, except in the world of make-believe. This is obvious from our behaviour in times of crisis. We expect to have a say about our destiny and are not prepared to leave it to be decided by others. We assume we have influence and power among the nations.

When I consider the nine years we have lived through since the second world war, my main feelings are two: pride in the great achievement of my country, concern that we may not secure the future we expect. It may seem that these two feelings are almost mutually exclusive and cannot animate the same mind at the same time. This has not been my experience. I have lived and continue to live with both these feelings about Britain. There is nothing special about my pride in the post-war achievement of Britain. I share the feelings of most of my fellow-citizens. But you know how our habits of understating what we think and

minimising what we feel often completely deceive people
from overseas. I sometimes think that when, in talking to
each other, we concentrate on the occasions when we have
done less than we hoped and things have not gone right
for us in the world, we almost deceive ourselves and miss
the great positive achievement of post-war Britain. It may
be that living outside Britain has made it easier for me to
see this, just as distance reveals a mountain rising clear
above the shoulders, valleys and forests which preoccupy
a nearer gaze.

After all, we have made a good record. After a six years'
war which, with the Commonwealth, we fought from first
to last, to which we devoted all we had, we emerged weak
and terribly strained. But we had not lost our unity or
vitality.

We have had enough vitality to transform the Indian
Empire into free nations of the Commonwealth; to embark
by decision of the electorate on a vast programme of social
experiment at home; to invent the concept of Atlantic
Union and join with others in making reality conform to
the idea; and to keep alive after the war something of the
war-time partnership with the United States so that we still
could encourage or restrain our friend.

We have had enough unity to steer clear of social disorder and incurable divisions in our community. Through
the resolute effort of the whole people we have achieved
a total of exports, year in, year out, which no official estimate, domestic or foreign, dared forecast. Together we have
endured fair shares of austerity under Cripps and relaxed
together under Butler when austerity was no longer needed.
And step by step we have improved the performance of our
whole economy until the pound sterling has again become
a desirable currency among the traders and bankers of
the world.

We have created a ballet equal to any there has been.
We have bred the first man to run a mile in under four
minutes. We have produced the leader whose genius

overcame Mount Everest. And there was a moment when we saw the achievement of Britain for what it is. In 1953, at the Coronation, we suddenly knew that we believed in ourselves. We had great cause for pride.

But it is my concern about which I wish to talk. I want to tell you how it arose, what are the considerations which gave it strength, and what are the lines of thought and action along which it seems to me an answer can be found. I am clear how it arose. It came into being as I looked back at Britain across the Atlantic and argued the case for Britain with my American friends. Since the war we have lived through years of acute political controversy between the two great parties. After the 1945 election the British people has returned first one and then the other party to power by narrow margins. Throughout the period the extent and the cost of action to realise the principles of the Welfare State, the issue of nationalisation, the repeated crises of the economy—these have been the things which attracted public attention and captured the headlines. Because opinion in the country was deeply divided about them, the full force of Parliamentary debate was concentrated on these questions.

But I also noticed something else. There were other matters on which we took action which by contrast attracted little debate or notice. They were not controversial.

There was the atomic energy programme. At the end of the war the Americans had full-scale plant for the development of atomic energy from the raw material to the finished product. We had nothing. We had agreed it should all happen over there and had contributed to it. It was obvious that possession of the secrets of the large-scale production of atomic energy would be of the greatest importance in the future for peace as well as for war. At great cost in scarce resources we embarked upon a full programme with nothing but green fields and grey matter.

The war also made us give up the development and manufacture of new types of large aircraft. When peace came, we were years behind our American competitors. Again diverting scarce resources from immediate needs, we took action which has come to fruition in the last two or three years. Today our engines and some of our aircraft lead the world.

In the field of foreign affairs there was a crucial decision —the Berlin airlift. We decided, almost without discussion, to take our share with the Americans. And it was crucial: it involved the risk of war; it was a turning-point in the post-war history of Europe. We had a leading part in originating the Atlantic Pact and we accepted its consequences. Today four British divisions stand on the soil of Europe in peace time, an astonishing revolution from all past traditions. On this, too, the nation has not been divided.

Throughout these years the decision of the British Government has been to restore the position of sterling and make it again an international currency of known stability and strength. The political parties have been in agreement on this basic issue.

Why should these decisions, all of them of first-class importance and with far-reaching consequences, have occasioned so little discussion and debate? It is because they all flowed from an accepted principle: they did not derive from the area in which party political differences were alive and real. Nor is the principle obscure or difficult to identify. It can be stated very simply. Britain is going to continue to be what she has been, a Great Power. This is something the British people assume and act upon. Once they see that some action or decision is required by this first principle of national policy, they accept it and do not question further.

I do not think I need discuss the exact definition of a Great Power. We all have a good idea. A nation which is a Great Power has a certain range of choice and manoeuvre in world affairs and can take an effective part in the great decisions which affect the course of history. The action of a Great Power can decisively affect the fate of other Great

Powers in the world. It is in this sense that we assume that our future will be of one piece with our past and that we shall continue as a Great Power. What is noteworthy is the way that we take this for granted. It is not a belief arrived at after reflection by a conscious decision. It is part of the habit and furniture of our minds: a principle so much one with our outlook and character that it determines the way we act without emerging itself into clear consciousness. I think that almost all of us take this view of Britain for granted. I certainly have done so.

Yet what we have taken for granted has not been taken for granted abroad. This is one of the things I discovered in the United States. I was repeatedly challenged to justify my view of Britain's future, most often by good friends of ours who desired to provoke a reassuring response. But sometimes the questions went deeper. They sprang from indifferent or hostile sources, and by implication denied what I assumed. I had to fight for my belief: I was forced to think hard about what I had taken for granted.

Why were so many Americans sceptical about the continued ability of Britain to act as a Great Power? In the earlier years after the war they pointed in evidence to obvious signs of weakness. There was our economic exhaustion and dependence on aid from abroad. There was the end of the Indian Empire. For, while Americans applauded the constructive quality and the timing of our bold decision, they also saw it marked a major diminution of Britain's power.

But, beyond these political and economic considerations about Britain, it was felt by many Americans that a new pattern was emerging in world affairs. It was the age of nations on a continental scale. There were really only two of them, only two Great Powers: the United States and Russia. I was often reminded of De Tocqueville's words written more than 100 years ago. You will remember how he speaks of the unnoticed growth of these two nations while the world was busy looking at other things and how therefore the world noticed their existence and their power almost at the same time. 'Their starting point', he goes on, 'is different and their courses are not the same: yet each of them seems marked out by the will of heaven to sway the destinies of half the globe'. The antiquity and aptness of these observations have given some Americans a feeling of certainty. In the new age the United States and the Union of Soviet Socialist Republics alone really counted.

The judgement that Britain is no longer a Great Power is illustrated with force and clarity in a book, *Politics among Nations*, by Professor Hans Morgenthau of the University of Chicago. I quote from it because it is widely used as a text-book in American universities and is therefore read by many young Americans:

Today Great Britain's friendship is no longer of decisive importance. . . . Even as late as the second world war, the neutrality of Great Britain or its alignment with Germany and Japan instead of with the United Nations might easily have meant for the latter the difference between victory and defeat. Now, in view of the probable trends in the technology of warfare and the distribution of power between the United States and the Soviet Union, it may well be that the attitude of Great Britain in an armed conflict between these two powers would not decisively affect the ultimate outcome. In the metaphorical language of the balance of power one might say, rather crudely but not without truth, that, while in the Russian scale there is a weight of seventy, the weight of the American scale amounts to a hundred, of which seventy is the United States' own strength, ten that of Great Britain, and the remainder that of the other actual or prospective allies. Thus, even if the British weight were removed from the American scale and placed into the Russian, the heavier weights would still be in the American scale.

I encountered these opinions as I lived and worked in the United States. They were held by some, not by all, not by a majority, of Americans. And I could tell from conversations with my diplomatic colleagues that these views about the future of Britain were entertained in many other countries besides the United States: they were in no way special or peculiar to the Americans. What matters is not the country of origin but the strong negative quality of these beliefs. It was to this that I reacted. The more I worked to find an effective response with which to overcome the opposing arguments, the more convinced I became of two things. I became convinced of what I had previously taken for granted, that Britain is a Great Power and has it in her to continue to be so; and I also became convinced that I, and, I think, most of us in this country, have not yet thought out the cumulative effect of the vast changes in the world upon our country and therefore are not yet clear what we must do to make what we take for granted unchallengeably evident to all.

This, then, is my concern: and this is the story of its origin and growth. I am concerned lest Britain, by failing to take thought in time and failing to act in time, miss the future we expect and assume.

It is worth while reminding ourselves of the scale and pace of the world's change. I was born in 1905 and am nearly fifty years old. Many of you will be younger, some much younger, and will not remember the Edwardian era into which I was born and in which I passed my childhood before the first world war. The scale and the pace of the change can be illustrated by looking at a few of the things that have happened in my lifetime. I recite them not to lament a golden age when the power, prestige and influence of Britain stood at high noon. The important thing is to see ourselves as we are and not as we were; to see Europe, Asia, the United States, the British Commonwealth and Empire as they are, not as they were; to see the balance of power in the world, of military power, of economic power, of the power of creative ideas, as it is, not as it was.

This is as difficult as it sounds easy. The psychologists have told us that the sensations and impressions received in very early childhood exercise a determining role in the broad attitudes we have to life in later years. I think in some ways they exaggerate: but not in all. If anyone suddenly says to me 'The map of the world', the picture which instantly rises in my mind is Mercator's projection from my 1912 atlas, with so much of the world coloured in one flat wash of red, the many overseas dependencies of Britain, the British Empire. Such vivid associations almost unconsciously colour one's approach to world affairs and the place of Britain. Today these associations are misleading and damaging to Britain's prospects if we let ourselves be influenced by them. Kipling's Empire is no longer there. Something else is there instead. The kind of scene we look at today was described simply and memorably by Her Majesty the Queen on that Christmas afternoon when she spoke to her Commonwealth from New Zealand:

Every one of its nations can be justly proud of what it has built for itself on its own soil. But their greatest achievement, I suggest, is the Commonwealth itself; and that owes much to all of them. Thus formed, the Commonwealth bears no resemblance to the empires of the past. It is an entirely new conception, built on the highest qualities of the spirit of man —friendship, loyalty, and the desire for freedom and peace.

The British Empire has been transformed in my lifetime: but so has much else. When I was a child the centre of the artistic, the scientific, the intellectual life of the world was in Europe. The balance of power between the major European nations was at the same time the world balance. The destinies of the whole Old World were swayed by European nations. The peoples of the New World were absorbed in their own expansion and development and had little interest in world affairs. Men were confident that the world was becoming an orderly place. There were wars, but for 100 years they had been successfully localised. International trade flourished. Each decade seemed to yield its own evidence of the reality of progress.

Now Europe is no longer pre-eminent: it is divided,

impoverished and weak. The balance of world power lies outside Europe. The poles of international tension are Washington and Moscow. The United States and the Soviet Union seem to dwarf all other nations: their shadows lie across the entire globe. The west has retreated from Asia where large new experiments in self-government have begun; there are stirrings and unrest in Africa. The old system of international trade has broken down and no substitute has yet been built up to take its place. By comparison with the world of my childhood, we live in a divided, fearful, suspicious world. One third of the population of the globe is withdrawn by the Communists from normal intercourse. Ideas are at war in the world and we are all expected to take sides.

When I was a child Britain stood foremost among the nations. Accumulated wealth, geographical position, the British Navy, the British Indian Army, the strong patriotism of the British people assured and buttressed this position. In the last forty years, mainly because of two world wars, change has been rapid. We are not now the most powerful nation in the world. We owe great debts abroad. The aeroplane, the guided missile, the atomic bomb have destroyed the privileged immunity of the island. Britannia does not rule the waves alone, and the British Indian Army is no more. Only the spirit of the British people survives the years unchanged.

These are all facts: they illustrate the dimensions and the speed of the great changes in the world. But to my mind they are significant in relation to the issue I have raised. Taken together they suggest the changed conditions of Britain's greatness. Until forty years ago the traditional foreign policy of Britain was generally understood by the people and was for the most part decisive in the actual conduct of foreign affairs. It depended on the power and prestige of Britain. It was based on our independence and freedom to act as we chose: an independence and freedom given by geography, augmented by wealth, and secured by armed might. The policy was to maintain the balance of power in Europe and keep command of the seas. Our position was assured so long as no one nation became predominant on the continent of Europe and no foreign fleets could challenge ours.

In relation to the world balance of power centred on Europe we thought of ourselves as sitting by the tongue of the balance, watching the weights in the scales and always ready, if the weights in one scale seemed dangerously to outweigh those in the other, to throw ourselves in and restore the balance between the scales. This was a position of isolation—splendid isolation, it was called: a position only possible for a nation so powerful that it could afford to stand outside alliances and combinations until it decided the moment had come to intervene.

Consider the situation now and the contrast that it makes. The dominant characteristic of the world today is its division. On the one side there is the compact group of Communist states stretching from the Elbe to Vladivostok, from Archangel to Canton and Pyongyang. On the other there are the nations who oppose the opportunist aggression of the Communists, and those who hope, like Sweden or Switzerland, India or Indonesia, not to be compelled by events to take their stand. In this divided world no nation is so powerful as to be able to stand aside in safety. The weights of the Soviet Union and of China with those of the satellite Communist states lie heavy in one scale. The counterweight in the second scale is mainly given by the United States, Britain and the British Commonwealth, and the nations of western Europe. Not only Britain, but the United States and the Soviet Union too, are in the balance, weights in the scales whether it is liked or not.

This in epitome is the great change of the forty years. We are no longer free to intervene and choose our partners as and when we wish. If anyone doubts this, let him look at the Atlantic Pact: he will see combined and associated together in defence Britain and the United States, Canada from the Commonwealth, and a group of the nations of western Europe, all weights in the same scale.

What, then, are the conditions of Britain's greatness in this new conjuncture of international affairs? They lie in the effectiveness of our association with our friends. This means that we accept the permanence of these associations and clearly realise that the basis of our traditional policy is gone. We shall continue as a Great Power as, within these associations, we take the initiative, persuade our friends and lead. Our resources, spiritual and material, must be so strong that our friends will accept this from us and consult us in advance whenever they have an idea or want to act. It is as good partners that we shall maintain the freedom and independence of a Great Power and play a major role in the great decisions of history.

But all this depends on one thing: that we deal with our friends as they are and not as they were, not letting memories blur our perception of present reality. Otherwise we shall not be effective. Our enduring associations are within the Commonwealth, with the United States and with the nations of western Europe. All three are greatly changed from what they were. They are the three circles of our life and power.

II

BRITAIN AND THE NEW COMMONWEALTH

How easily the words come together on our lips: 'Britain and the British Commonwealth'. The idea for which they stand is comfortable and familiar: the fact to which they refer solid and comforting. We feel differently about our relations within the Commonwealth and those we have with the rest of the world. When we deal with the other members of the Commonwealth we are dealing with our own family. They are tied to us by kinship or long association. We understand each other, we get on, we settle things within the family. There are differences: what family is without them? But they are not allowed to disturb our mutual understanding.

Most of us, I think, have felt rather like this in recent years. After all the Commonwealth has grown out of our own history, out of ourselves and our activities in the world. There is a natural affinity between us all: there is a continuity which has not been broken by the quick growth of independence. The Commonwealth is a reassuring, friendly club to which to belong.

I suggest that this attitude is based on half-truths and is, therefore, misleading and dangerous. It leaves out of account the most striking characteristic of the Commonwealth to-day, that it is a great political experiment of the most challenging and unfamiliar nature. Never before has there been anything like it in the world. First of all, the great combinations of peoples which history has known have been based on fear or force. There are many cases where fear of another power has induced an alliance or confederation. There are many where the force exerted by one nation has compelled others to obey its will and work in combination with it. Neither fear nor force unites the

Commonwealth. It is built on the positive foundation of
mutual advantage and consent. The experiment is as recent
as the sovereign independence of the member nations.

Secondly, one of the great tides in world affairs is the
ebb of the political power and influence of the West from
the East. All through Asia new nations have been coming
into existence—nations sensitive to the least hint of interfer-
ence and suspicious of the good faith of the West. Division
has come in place of domination, a division no less important to the future of the world than that between the communist bloc and the free peoples. The British Commonwealth alone has bridged this gulf and built a highroad
across it. Whenever I stand back and look at this, not in
terms of historical development but in terms of the world
today, it seems to me an astonishing experiment, challenging
the whole trend of things, as constructive as it is bold.

But we have to see the Commonwealth and our position
and relationships within it as they are. For here we have
the fundamental condition of our continuing greatness: by
itself it is not enough but it is basic. Without the Commonwealth we cannot continue as a Great Power and the continued existence of this great experiment is not guaranteed
or secure: it has to be achieved, and by far the greatest
responsibility rests on us.

Little argument is needed to show the necessity of the
Commonwealth to Britain's continuing greatness. It is a
truth which the British people have intuitively perceived:
they do not require a demonstration. What is this small
island with its 50,000,000 inhabitants if it has to go it
alone? It is one of two things, an off-island of Europe or
an off-island of the United States of America. In either
case our destinies would be decided on the mainland, on
the continent of Europe or in the continental United States.
If we wished to maintain a standard of living anything like
that we now enjoy and have any voice in our own future,
we should find ourselves forced in the long run to coalesce
ever more closely with one of the continental systems. We

should face absorption into Europe or becoming in effect a dependency of the United States.

The British people have reached definite opinions on singularly few of the great issues that have confronted their country since the war. But on these matters they have made their views known with absolute clarity. They do not want to become absorbed into Europe; they do not wish to live in dependence on the United States. All the more reason then for making a success of the Commonwealth. This is the relationship which enables us to play in the big league with the continental powers. It is success here which permits us to stand out of the queue and fill the role of a Great Power, which gives us reasonable independence among our friends and a part in the great decisions. This is why it is vital that we see the Commonwealth and Britain's job in it as clearly as we can.

I myself began to see all this a little more clearly while I was Ambassador in Washington. So I think the best thing I can do is to take some of the things we all know about the Commonwealth and illustrate from my experience how they came alive for me and the difference my new perspective made.

The nations of the Commonwealth are free and equal: they are all sovereign states. This was impressed on me the very first day I arrived in Washington. There was a group at the station to welcome me. It included the Chief of Protocol from the American State Department, British Embassy staff, and seven Commonwealth Ambassadors. I suddenly realised that there were already six representatives of His Majesty in Washington, as well as the Indian Ambassador whose Government recognised the King as Head of the Commonwealth. From one point of view, and it was a real one, I was the junior Ambassador of His Majesty in the United States.

I have another recollection. You will remember the visit paid to Canada by Princess Elizabeth with the Duke of Edinburgh before she became the Queen. The Princess was invited by the President of the United States to come to Washington. At first I assumed without thought that a British Princess was coming, but my distinguished Canadian colleague, the late Hume Wrong, made it clear to me that in Canada the Princess was a Canadian Princess and in Canada's view a Canadian Princess would soon be crossing the border, I realised as I had never done before that the Princess was not only a Princess in the United Kingdom, but also the Princess of six other countries.

The members of the Commonwealth are independent nations: we all know that. But before I worked with the other Commonwealth representatives in Washington my ideas about this independence were rather negative. I knew the other members were no longer dependent on Britain— they were free to decide whether to stay in the Commonwealth or not. But now I learned that this independence had a very positive character. The other members each had their own foreign policy, political and economic. Canada, Australia, India or Pakistan: the Government of the United States listened with great attention to their views. At different times these nations exercised real influence in the formation of American policy. In fact Britain belonged to a club each member of which was positively shaping its own destiny.

I was interested to see that the special correspondent for *The Times* on the royal tour formed much the same general impression about Australia. He wrote:

The war and its aftermath have transformed Australia's isolation at the end of the world into a lively international concern, especially with the affairs of Asia, where many diplomatic posts have been manned that did not exist before 1939. Canberra, indeed, is the centre of intensive diplomatic activity, and the old American quip that nations of the British Commonwealth regularly 'wrote home to mother' but rarely to one another could no longer be made at the expense of the Australian foreign service, which has become a prolific letter writer to all the relatives, none more than to Canada.

Again, we all know that the Commonwealth is a unity. But in Washington I saw how that unity worked. Every fortnight except in the summer the eight Ambassadors of the Commonwealth met in our Embassy to exchange views and consult informally together. We discussed everything: the movement of affairs in the world, the latest phase of American policy—and the opinions of our different countries about them. We did not mince words. Even difficulties between individual members, like Kashmir, were regularly talked over by all of us, including India and Pakistan, with conviction but without heat. Further, the discussions took place between like-minded people who shared a common political tradition. No one had to insist on the freedom of his country because nobody ever questioned it. We had a common approach. We accepted common standards. We had forbearance, which is essential between members of a continuing club when they differ.

What did I get out of this experience? A new view of the power and positive influence of the Commonwealth countries in the world. A better conception of what the equality and independence of our partners means to them and to us. I could see that any notion of Britain as a mother with a number of sons, now all legally of age but still a trifle undergraduateish in outlook, is totally mistaken. We are dealing with equals. They expect to be consulted on matters of common interest before we act and not told about it afterwards. If we forget for a moment and act in terms of an older relationship, the reminder that we get is quick and unambiguous. It is because these truths have been applied by us at recent Commonwealth Economic Conferences that they have been so successful. This was particularly so with the conference at Sydney, although in the opinion of those who took part its constructive quality and success were matched only by the dullness of the final communiqué.

But all this is a static analysis of the Commonwealth. It gives no clue to why it works or what are the factors which can hold it together and make it work in the future. What is it, in the expressive American phrase, that makes the Commonwealth tick? The backward glance of reminiscence suggests that the clue is to be found in common origins and common history. Some nations of the Commonwealth are linked to Britain by kinship, others by long association, all by sentiment. Above all there is the Crown embodying the principles of continuity and unity within the Commonwealth and as such accepted by all the partners. For most of them it is more. It is a shared institution, standing high above the waves of change and political controversy.

These are high arguments. No one who followed the royal tour of the Queen and her Consort can doubt the supreme importance to the Commonwealth of the loyal affection which centred on the Queen wherever she went. But there is no disloyalty in saying that this alone is not a full explanation of what makes the Commonwealth work. The mistake would be to expect more of the Crown than can possibly be given. And much the same holds good of the ties of sentiment, real though they are, and the facts of kinship and contact from which they flow.

Aristotle thought pleasure might be likened to the bloom on the cheeks of youth. It was, so to speak, a quality which supervened on others which were prerequisite. So the theologians thought of grace as the perfection of nature: it supervened on the natural activities of man as a quality of a higher order. Common origins remembered, ties of sentiment, the Crown itself are all higher-order links within the Commonwealth. If they are to exercise their strong influence, they presuppose what I am going to call, rather clumsily, first-order links.

What are these? They are economic and political, links of mutual advantage, necessary for the successful working of the Commonwealth though far from sufficient to give it its peculiar strength and quality. And yet these links of economic and political advantage are strong. Britain is a great natural market for the foodstuffs and raw materials produced by the other Commonwealth nations. Britain sends in return what countries actively developing their resources naturally need, manufactured goods and capital. In a prosperous year we export to our fellow-members goods to the value of near £1,000 millions. But the political advantages are equally direct and simple; for the other members as well as for Britain. Each becomes more, has more influence on the course of world affairs, a more effective say in the great political and strategic issues of our time, more opportunity of effective action in international efforts to increase trade and raise the standard of living, because of belonging to the Commonwealth. The advantages are not one way: they are mutual. That is why they offer a basis on which to build for a long future.

What makes the Commonwealth work is a complex of motives in which each element reinforces the others. The elements relate to very different qualities and needs in human nature. For this reason in combination they are both strong and supple. Perhaps that is why some people in our country go to an extreme. They realise that Britain cannot go it alone in the present world: they see, too, that the prospect of her continued greatness is bound up with the Commonwealth. Why should not Britain make her great aim the strengthening of the Commonwealth and in its ever closer unity find the full realisation of her inheritance? They have a vision of Britain and the Commonwealth, friendly with all but dependent on none, finding together all the strength they need.

This may be an attractive picture. I shall not stop to argue that. The point is that things cannot turn out that way. This is certain, it is not a matter of opinion. The first proof is in the existence of the Atlantic Pact, acclaimed the corner-stone of our defence by Conservative and Labour Governments alike. Two members of the Commonwealth have thought it right and necessary to combine for the purposes of mutual defence with the United States across the Atlantic and western European nations across the

Channel. The combination is long-term, not short-term. In this divided and dangerous world Britain and Canada know that their fortunes are bound up with those of nations outside the Commonwealth.

It is worth taking the matter a little further. I am clear that a policy of going it alone would split and destroy the Commonwealth if it were ever submitted seriously for decision. It would be unacceptable to both the Asian and the western members. In the last few years it has been obvious that India is devoting sustained effort to cultivating friendship with its far-eastern neighbours. India would accept no proposal or commitment which would prevent or limit this broad policy. And Pakistan has links which it hopes to strengthen with the Moslem peoples of the Middle and Near East. Any proposal likely to thwart a natural ambition to become the leader of a group of middle-eastern states would not be entertained.

Equally, the western members would never consent. Think of Canada in relation to the United States: 3,000 miles of frontier, a population about equal to that of New York State, common defence problems, strong ties in finance, trade and industry, an old, enduring and reciprocated friendship. Think of American participation in the development of Canadian oil and the iron ore of Labrador, the joint interest in the St. Lawrence Waterway. The future of Canada, while all her own, must be linked to that of the United States.

Then there is the attitude of Australia and New Zealand. They could not do without their Pacific neighbour, the United States: they have said so in the Anzus Pact. This pact is new. Let us be frank: it has surprised and pained many people in Britain that Australia and New Zealand should enter into such an understanding with the United States but without us. This is precisely the sort of issue in Commonwealth affairs which we need to look at with eyes unclouded by older memories.

In 1950 the North Koreans launched their deliberate

attack. Nations whose strategic interests lay immediately in the south Pacific had to revise their ideas. At the same time a liberal peace treaty was being negotiated with the Japanese, who less than ten years before had fought their way to the outskirts of Australia. Australians and New Zealanders both felt a new urgency about defence. They remembered the second world war and the collapse of preconceived defence plans when Singapore fell. It was the American armed forces which checked Japan. Australia and New Zealand saw that the first power in the Pacific was the United States. When the Korean war made prospects across the Pacific uncertain and insecure, it was natural for these two Pacific members of the Commonwealth to enter into understandings about the common defence with the United States. The Anzus Pact acknowledges a vital strategic relationship.

The other nations of the Commonwealth are in the same case as Britain. Our future, like our past, is bound up with that of our neighbours in western Europe and the United States. The evidence of two world wars and of the Atlantic Pact is final. The strength and vitality of the Commonwealth does not lie in the separation of its members from their neighbours. It is not that sort of exclusive club. It is its nature to reach out, not to retreat like a snail into its shell. Rightly conceived, the connections of interest and policy which each Commonwealth nation enjoys with its neighbours are a source of strength to the whole, not of weakness. They contribute to the effective working of the Commonwealth because they increase the understanding and the influence of each member in its region. And between them the members cover five continents of the world.

This then in outline is how I find myself thinking of the Commonwealth today. But the picture still lacks an essential part. The position of Britain and her function within the Commonwealth are in the last resort decisive, for she is its heart and focus. The strings of the Commonwealth relationship go out from her and return to her. She has laid down the conditions of the great experiment.

There is a danger that Britain, while having successfully avoided one trap, might fall into another. We have avoided the dangers of holding back on the equality and independence of our partners. When the old relationships were past, we have not fallen into the trap of still trying to impose our will. We have fulfilled the first, the negative element, in our role. The danger is that we leave things at that, and do not see our positive function. The second trap is that we can go on being so anxious to avoid the first that we neglect our duty to lead. The Commonwealth cannot get on and succeed without a leader, and there is no one except ourselves who can give a lead. What is more, this is expected of us. Ask anyone who has been at recent Commonwealth conferences: we are expected to take the initiative, and if we are not ready to do so, the conference stalls.

We are expected to give the lead but we are expected to do so on merit. None of our partners is going to accept what we say on trust because it is what the British say or because of British prestige or British industrial power. We have got to take the initiative and do it so well that the other members of the Commonwealth welcome the British initiative and are glad to acknowledge Britain's position as a good and effective chairman of the club's activities. This is why the comfortable easy-going view of the Commonwealth we are prone to take is misleading and dangerous for us. If the great experiment with all its constructive possibilities in the world is to succeed, the responsibility in the last resort rests chiefly with Britain. We need to do things we do not particularly like doing if we are to play our part: we shall have to take thought and articulate some of the general aims of long-term policy: we shall have deliberately to take decisions and devote resources to the Commonwealth: we shall have to go on, as the British Government has been doing, working really hard at our job.

Exercising leadership in Commonwealth affairs does

involve heavy calls on our resources, spiritual and material. We must also be clear about that. On the economic side we have to find money, goods and ideas. Capital for our developing partners; goods to exchange for raw materials and food; ideas to keep policy about commerce and currency moving on sensible lines. We have been and are supplying capital, but not enough. The target given by the Chancellor of the Exchequer was £300 millions a year. Our performance is a good deal short of that, and it matters: for the supply of capital is one of the links between Britain and the other members, and if the link is weak, it transmits weakness to the other links as surely as, if it is strong, it reinforces their strength. It is very important that in the future the developing nations of the Commonwealth should not look elsewhere for most of the capital they need.

Again, we send great quantities of manufactured goods, but requirements are changing and we have to meet and anticipate the change. Nowadays part of the definition of nationhood is industrial development. The other members of the Commonwealth are no exception. They are industrialising themselves as fast as they can, at times almost faster than they can afford. But they will not stop: it is part of being free and equal, independent nations. As secondary industries spring up overseas, and primary too, the type of British exports has to change. It has been changing fast since the war. We have to build and sell capital equipment and complex long-lasting engineering goods, at a price, of a quality, with delivery dates competitive with our rivals in the United States and Germany.

We have to think out sensible policies for commerce and currency. In this lecture I will say only this: at all costs we must avoid clinging to outworn ideas. There is a current example of what I mean. A group of people in Britain, rightly seeing the importance of maintaining and increasing trade within the Commonwealth, advocate a policy of increased imperial preference. It is pointless to argue the merits of this proposal for the simple reason that it is out of date and has no chance. I am under the impression that we have raised the matter two or three times at Commonwealth conferences and have got nowhere. At the end of the last discussion the Rhodesias were willing, New Zealand reminiscent, Australia oracular, and all the rest opposed: Canada absolutely, on principle and on expediency, for it would involve living next door to a violently opposed United States; the Asian countries because the idea reminded them of colonialism and imperialism.

Beyond this there is the political side of things. In defence we have to continue to be a firm base able to give assistance as well as receive it if we are attacked. But above all we have to take views which are large and sane on the great issues which divide the world, the Communist bloc, nationalist Asia and the future of colonial peoples. We have to show that in our relations with the United States we can combine firm friendship with frankness and evolve joint policies which do not entail our giving in where we should not. I believe, to sum up, that what will induce our partners in the Commonwealth to expect and welcome the leadership of Britain is the conviction, sustained by example, that we labour with intelligence and determination for the sanity of the world.

III

BRITAIN AND THE UNITED STATES: THE TRIALS OF INTERDEPENDENCE

SINCE the war we have felt comfortable about the Commonwealth. But we have felt increasingly uncomfortable about our relationship with the United States. In the last four years, especially, we have been disturbed about what the Americans were doing or might do.

I think I should make my own position clear at the outset. I believe that in their dealings with other nations the American people intend good and not evil, and I believe they want peace, not war. There are some who will think this nonsense. I am sure it is not; and my conviction is based on years of negotiation and discussion with Americans on a great variety of topics. There is no shallower delusion than the idea that we could get along without the United States, or indeed that the United States could get along without us: our interdependence is a fact. I am glad that our Governments since the war have accepted this fact and acted on it. For I also believe that close and effective co-operation between Britain and the United States is the basic condition of an orderly world, the best chance of avoiding another world war, and our hope of peace.

I do not imagine for one moment that these convictions are peculiar to me. I suppose them to be not very different from what most of you really believe. But many people in Britain have rather lost sight of them because in recent years they have been overlaid and obscured by anxieties about the United States. I hope in this lecture to persuade you that it would be stupid to allow these nagging fears and doubts to determine our attitude to the Americans.

There is no doubt that close association with the United States is necessary to Britain. The unity of the Commonwealth, our economic welfare, the defence of Britain alike demand it. There is no need to go on with the argument. Self-interest binds us to the United States. But it is a two-way relationship. The self-interest of the United States is also involved. The great aim of American foreign policy in recent years has been to keep the free world large and not to let it shrink to the New Hemisphere, perhaps even to the North American continent. No thinking American today can be an isolationist—can possibly contemplate the isolation of his continental island from the resources and the teeming populations of the three continents of the Old World. For this the United States needs us. It is only in co-operation with Britain, the linchpin of the Commonwealth, the strong island athwart the approaches to western Europe, that American foreign policy can succeed.

What reason commands, the heart approves. We share with the Americans a common language and a common heritage. Countless British families have their cousins in the United States. The ties of kinship and sentiment are real, and they powerfully reinforce the bonds of interest. They make it natural for us to believe that our future is bound up with the Americans. Yet if action is the test of effective belief, some of us do not pass the test. The Americans, some feel, make themselves so difficult to get on with. There should be close and harmonious association but there are too many obstacles. It is risky to be too close to them.

To allow one's feelings to take charge like this is to fail to see things as they are. Positive and continuing co-operation with the United States is the second condition of Britain maintaining her position as a Great Power. We are thrown together in the same scale of the global balance of power. If we want to stand out of the queue, not to be committed by the decisions of others and dragged at the heel of events, we must stand out by the positive quality of our relations with our friends, and particularly with the United States of America.

As it takes two to make a quarrel, it takes two to get on well. I have been talking as if the Americans made all the difficulties and this is not so. The Americans feel that we make a good many difficulties for them, and if I were addressing an American audience I should be expected to deal with them. But as I am talking to you I propose to examine a little more closely the difficulties many people in Britain feel about the United States. I think there are four and I name them in ascending order of importance: the frictions of association in the same scale of the world balance, the discomforts of the passage of power, McCarthyism, and the fear that the United States will land us in a third world war.

Both countries feel the frictions of association. Both nations have been accustomed to stand outside the balance of power and judge, each for itself, the moment of intervention. The habit of mind persists after the facts have changed. Each nation at times resents the other's influence in modifying policy. That the British should have to make allowance for American views and the Americans for British feels like an undue limitation on freedom of action.

Occasions of irritation have been increased because since the war the British and American Governments have been ahead of popular feeling in recognising and accepting the changed positions of their countries. There is more mutual consultation over a wider range of matters, a more deliberate attempt to reconcile divergent views, more common action than either we or the Americans have ever had before with any nation. As a result, some Americans fear their Administration is too much under the influence of the British. Some British insist that Britain must be detached from the American sphere of influence. Last summer a member of the American Administration thought it wise to state publicly that Britain had no veto over American actions. Here we have had the complaint that Britain was falling in behind the United States. These frictions are really problems of adjustment, of getting rid of outdated habits and living in the world of today. There is nothing that time and effort cannot cure.

Then there are the discomforts of the passage of power. When I was a child the seat of world power was London, now it is Washington. We are not used to change, we do not like it. We do not like needing economic or defence aid. We observe the marked difference in wealth between us and American visitors or Air Force personnel posted to Britain, and it irks us. We were brought up sharp when we suddenly realised that an American had been chosen as Admiral of the Atlantic. It is strange to us to find that all our international problems now have an extra dimension, an American dimension. In the Middle East, in south Asia, in south-east Asia it is the same: we find the Americans everywhere, active everywhere, promoting American policies.

The facts are as stated. Our feelings have not caught up with them. The change has been too rapid, just as it has been too rapid for the Americans. They are not used to a position in the world they did not seek. Most of them are genuinely reluctant to wear the mantle of leadership. They long for the simple days when they did not have to bother about the world's problems but pursued their destiny in the seclusion of their continent. Our discomforts, like their nostalgia, spring from incomplete adaptation to change: they are real but not incurably grave.

The third difficulty is McCarthyism; it belongs to a different category. One can understand the horror with which the American people discovered that the American way of life was not proof against the enemy within. The discovery that American communists had been able to penetrate departments of the Administration; the fact that Americans would undertake espionage on behalf of a foreign power; these things came as an immense shock to American pride and a blow to inner confidence and the sense of security. How deep the wound went can be judged from the amazing career Senator McCarthy has founded on its exploitation.

It is a tragedy that so many Americans have remained

unaware of the damage done by the Senator to the reputation of the United States in the world. He has made great numbers of people in Europe and Asia change their minds about the United States and lose confidence in the quality and future of American democracy. He has made it easier to lump the Soviet Union and the United States together as the two great threats to the peaceful progress of mankind. This defeat for the United States has occurred because the Senator in his investigations denied the ordinary rights of the individual in a democratic society to those whom he attacked, and because he used his official position to substitute with impunity insults and innuendo for proof. His methods, their contagious power, his apparent toleration by the American people, and the large volume of support he found among them have profoundly impressed and depressed many people in Britain naturally friendly to the United States.

I know that the conduct and career of Senator McCarthy raise issues of principle. I do not wish to minimise the sinister and anarchic character of his techniques. But I am sure that the United States cannot be judged wholly or mainly by McCarthyism and its effects. There has never been any evidence that the Senator might dominate the United States. To do that he would need a published political testament or an organisation. But the Senator has no positive doctrine; he leads no movement or party. And in the last few months signs have accumulated that his star has passed the zenith. It is true that McCarthyism goes beyond McCarthy. But it is also true that opposition to it has been voiced from the beginning and is increasing. I am certain that it would take far more than we have seen to undermine permanently the principles of individual freedom which were written into the American Constitution and have formed the living tradition of the United States for nearly 200 years. American democracy has vitality and toughness, though in its frightened response to the enemy within it has done things it will wish undone.

Last comes what I consider to be by far the greatest difficulty: the widespread fear that the United States will get us and others into a third world war. I am not going to argue that this fear is completely baseless. I have too much respect for the instinct of the British people. Indeed, it must be admitted that the Americans appear to convict themselves out of their own mouths. Consider the critical period in December 1950 and January 1951: defeat in Korea, when Mr. Attlee flew to Washington to confer with President Truman. Consider when the French were suffering defeat in Indo-China, and Sir Winston Churchill and Sir Anthony Eden flew to Washington to confer with President Eisenhower. On each occasion distinguished members of the United States Government and of the American Armed Forces publicly demanded a more aggressive American policy in the Far East and publicly advocated the extension of the fighting by sea blockade and bombing from the air.

It was difficult not to believe that this was the voice of the United States Government. And yet on neither occasion did these extreme policies in fact prevail. The Korean war remained localised and the truce in Indo-China was accepted. What is the reason for this incoherence between words and action? Mr. James Reston, of The New York Times, suggested an answer in an article he wrote last July after the visit of President Syngman Rhee to Washington. Mr. Reston said:

Dr. Rhee is not the only world figure who has misjudged the temper of the American Government. There are many others, on both sides of the Iron Curtain, who have based their judgements of America on what Washington says, instead of on what Washington does. And it is a dangerous procedure.

Europe's image of America as a headstrong, reckless nation spoiling for a fight could not possibly be more inaccurate. There are many men in this city who want a bolder and more aggressive policy towards the Communists, and they catch many headlines. They argue with great sincerity, and some of them with great eloquence, but they do not win the big battles. . . . When the early rounds are over and they get to the finals, where the issue is war or breaking the alliance, they lose.

The senators, the admirals and the generals do not, then, speak for the President or for the United States. They are saying what they themselves happen to think.

The British tradition is that Her Majesty's Government speaks with one voice. Ministers and officials are alike expected, whenever they speak in public, to state the policy of the Government. If there is any doubt, a Parliamentary question is asked. In the United States the fabric of government has a looser texture. It is much easier for politicians and officials to give expression to their personal views, and they frequently do. This is the phenomenon of the many voices so baffling to the foreigner trying to determine the policy of the United States Government. The Americans are not similarly nonplussed. They take these statements for what they are: personal contributions to a general debate.

It is important to remember that the foreign policy of the United States, as revealed in the acts of successive Administrations, has had a remarkable consistency. Furthermore, in spite of the vigour with which sudden changes and extreme solutions have often been urged, it has been cautious and responsible.

These considerations take us some way with the fourth difficulty, but they do not take us far enough. During each of the Far Eastern crises there was a fair volume of popular support in the United States for extreme views. Is it likely that some time in the future there will be so much support for extensive military action in the Far East that the course of the United States will be determined by it?

In the Korean and Indo-Chinese crises an American passion and the American temperament combined to stir popular opinion. The passion is about the Chinese Communist Government. The Americans believe that from the time of the Boxer Indemnities to the Communist seizure of power their relations with China were a model of what the association between a modern industrialised nation and an ancient undeveloped country might be. They built hospitals, schools, and universities and manned them with hundreds of devoted American men and women. They sent to China something of the best in the American way of life, free from all taint of colonialism and imperialism. Then came the Communist revolution and the Chinese suddenly treated their best friends as their worst enemies. In Korea they killed many American troops. The Americans were very angry: they still are. They feel that these evil men should not go unpunished. This is the passion which gives support to violent action in the Far East.

By temperament most Americans are men of action. Faced with a situation they feel frustrated unless they are doing something about it. Time for them is an enemy to be overcome, not, as we British tend to think, an ally to work with. They find release in action, in getting over and done with it. During these crises in the Far East temperament combined with passion to support bold, aggressive action. Yet the combination was not strong enough. I am inclined to think that in the future, as in the past, unless the Chinese embark on reckless action, these two factors will not control American action in the Far East.

But there is a third factor to be considered. So far it has not been operative. If it were, the answer might well be different. During the last eight years the policy of the United States Government towards the Communist bloc has been one of containment. This name for the policy has recently been out of fashion and other phrases have been used to give a new look. The substance of the policy has not changed much. The third factor is an element in it. The object of the policy of containment is to increase the prospects of peace. The Americans believe this object is furthered if lines are drawn and it is made clear to friend and foe alike that aggression across these lines will be resisted, if necessary by war. That I take it is the significance of the Atlantic Pact; a line has been publicly drawn from Norway to Turkey. The Pacific Pacts with Japan, the Philippines, and Australia and New Zealand draw a line between the islands of the Pacific and the mainland of Asia. The United States supported the South-East Asia Treaty of collective defence as a first step of the same sort. The Americans attach great importance to this element in the general policy of containment. They think it decreases the chances of war happening by miscalculation or accident. Many of them would say that in their opinion if Britain had made her position clear to all parties before the first world war, it might never have happened.

The idea of drawing a line and telling everyone in advance what will happen if it is crossed suits the American outlook. It does not come so naturally to us. We prefer to deal with events as they arise and not be committed by answering hypothetical questions. We have been willing to commit ourselves in the Atlantic theatre and draw a line there. We did this when we signed the Atlantic Pact. But then it has been easy to see the mortal danger that can threaten us from Europe. We feel differently about the Far East. Whatever reason may say, it still feels far away. To the United States it does not. It is where the second group of neighbours live across the other ocean. Russia is there as in Europe, and China is there too. War has come twice to the United States in the last thirteen years from the Pacific theatre.

When we are anxious about the United States starting a third world war, and eye the troubled situation in the Far East with particular apprehension, this is the factor with which we have to reckon. We need not primarily concern ourselves about American anger with the Chinese or the impulsive American temperament. We have to deal with a reasoned view, strongly held, on how best to deal with the Communist bloc in the Atlantic and Pacific theatres, if the chances of world war are to be minimised. No doubt these considerations are familiar to the British Government and its advisers. I do not think they are to most of us. So there is a real possibility of misunderstanding and therefore mistrusting the American attitude to world war.

If this analysis of the fourth and greatest difficulty we have about the Americans is broadly right, then the best remedy is clear. We know that we cannot hold back from the Americans. Because we are both World Powers with interests, responsibilities and commitments in many parts of the world, we consult each other every day. That Britain should be effective in this close association is a condition of her continuing greatness. It is also the condition of enlarging her freedom from her greatest fear. From both points of view it is necessary that our initiative and our view should count when the great decisions are taken. I do not imply that this has not been the case in recent years. My concern is with the future, not the past. I know from my own experience that at the time of the Korean crisis our opinion counted and made a difference to what happened. I do not doubt that in the Indo-China crisis last summer the same was true.

What then can we do for the future? I think three things are important. The first is to remember that even on major issues there will be give and take between the partners. Both British and Americans find it difficult to remember this, for they are apt still to be influenced by patterns of thought which belong to an earlier period when their countries still possessed full independence in action. Further, we have to be articulate about our policies. This is necessary if we wish to persuade or give a lead. But it goes against the grain. We prefer even among ourselves to say less than we think. But the British and American backgrounds of thought are not the same. What is left to be understood is misunderstood. If I had to state what I thought the most prevalent single cause of misunderstanding and suspicion between the United States and Britain, I should name the failure to communicate the assumptions of a proposal.

Lastly, we need more than positive articulate policies. Every American is like the man from Missouri; he has to be shown that we can perform what we propose. If he judges our material resources are adequate to sustain our policy or in a joint effort to support our reasonable contribution, he will be much more likely to agree with us. The American judges persons and nations more by their present than their past and more by his estimate of their future than their present. If the British economy is strong and healthy and promises progress, the United States will attach a great deal more weight to what we say on foreign policy. We shall find we are listened to as a Great Power in proportion as we can maintain our proper part in the common defence and find fresh resources to devote to the development of undeveloped free nations. The American tradition has little knowledge of glorious failures. In the Anglo-American relationship British policy has to pass the test: can the British deliver?

I hope I have shown that close association with the United States is a strenuous exercise for the British. I hope, too, that you feel that the Americans are about like us in the blend of reason, feeling and prejudice in their make-up, even though their reasons, feelings and prejudices are different.

I end on a personal note. I have never felt any hesitation in arguing against an American view if I had a good case and was convinced they were wrong. Those with whom I argued might get impatient and irritated, even angry at being held up by talk when they wanted to act. But I got a hearing and a reasonable share of what I wanted. The American people in their own fashion share our belief in settling things by debate. In our debates with them we have nothing to lose and much to gain by being fearless and forthright.

IV

BRITAIN AND THE MAKING OF EUROPE

I THINK most of you would be surprised if I suggested that August 10, 1952, was likely to be regarded by future historians as the most important date in the post-war decade of western Europe. But that is what I think. Why? It was the day on which the Schuman Plan became a reality. And I believe that if I explain how I came to this opinion I shall shed light on the third condition of Britain continuing to be a Great Power, an effective relationship with western Europe.

We have paid particular attention to European affairs perhaps three times since the war. The first was in 1948 when we were quick to recognise the meaning of the Communist seizure of power in Czechoslovakia and the Russian blockade of the western sectors of Berlin. The second occasion was during the first two years of the Marshall Plan. It was the time when Britain was accused of dragging her feet. The Americans believed that the key to European recovery lay in economic integration, and they put pressure on Britain. Recently we have been uneasily aware of the drive and energy of the Germans and the speed with which they were regaining power and position.

These are the occasions when, prompted by experience and tradition, we have been alert to developments in Europe and their significance to us. For the rest, we have assumed that western Europe is still much the same as it was. When we look at the map, we see the old familiar names; when we travel on business, we find the same industries in the same cities; when we go on holiday, we re-visit the old familiar places. I am speaking of the British people, not of the British Government. It is true that the Government since the war has faithfully reflected the conviction of the electorate that

Britain must not be absorbed into Europe. But the Government has also paid increasing attention to what is new in European affairs. It has moved from early indifference to support of new projects.

But most of us have assumed that the Europe we knew so well continues today. I believe there is an important sense in which this assumption is mistaken. The old Europe of independent, quarrelling, sovereign nations is no longer fully alive. We have made this mistake because, on the whole, we have been uninterested in what has been happening in Europe since the war. Indeed, there is no subject of absolutely first-class importance to Britain on which the great majority of the British people have thought less and cared less.

With the Americans, oddly enough, it has been different. Both the Administration and the people have come to believe that Europe has changed. It is a remarkable fact that the Americans have looked on the attainment of European unity as a direct and major interest of the United States, one of the great objectives of their post-war diplomacy. I believe that the Americans have been right in their diagnosis of western Europe and we have been wrong. I do not mean that they have been wise in all that they have done or always well advised in their methods. But they have been right in the essentials, in their perception that the pattern of sovereign nation states no longer completely fits Europe's needs. They were not misled in their instinctive feeling of support for the idea of unity.

I have met a good many men and women from different countries of western Europe and my conversations have left me with one clear impression: there are large numbers of people there who are living provisionally. For most of us in this country it is very hard to enter into such a frame of mind. They regard the whole pattern of their lives as a temporary arrangement. The society to which they belong is one they accept for the time being. The aims and the purposes they pursue are simply adopted in the absence of

anything else. This attitude has more than one cause. There
is the keen perception of the established disorder of European life and the impotence of the individual to do anything
about it. At best this breeds resignation while waiting for
the next chapter of history to open. Who can look at a
divided Germany, a divided Europe, a disorder illustrated
and exemplified by the impossible situation of Berlin, without realising that the whole framework of life is provisional?
On top of this comes the decay of loyalty to the organised
societies of Europe, the historic nation-states. People feel
that they can no longer place all their hope and trust in
their particular sovereign nation. This has nothing to do
with lack of courage or weakness of will. It is not a matter
of conscious decision. It is a state of mind born of defeat,
occupation, and the gulf between those who collaborated
and those who resisted.

The belief that all life is provisional has received its
extreme and reflective expression in the philosophy of Exis-
tentialism. Men cannot hope to affect an irrational and
indifferent environment by what they do, so that it is
pointless to judge action by its results. There is no sense in
trying to build a better society or a more stable future. The
only quality that counts in human living is the intensity,
the freedom, with which we act. This is a negative, anarchic
philosophy, despairing of effort and endeavour.

The conviction of the provisional character of life is
deeply rooted in western Europe. It offers no foundation
on which to build. For this very reason, we in Britain should
give special attention to the things which have life in them.
It is from them and their encounter that the western Europe
of tomorrow will emerge. There are three such things:
communism, the movement for European unity, and Germany.

We know that communism offers hope to millions in
western Europe. It appeals both to extreme poverty and
to frustrated intelligence. For it seems to offer a key to the
problems of human society: it is a doctrine which appears

to give a solution to all major problems at once. Today one quarter of the electorate in France, one third in Italy, vote communist. These communist parties are the greatest asset of the Soviet Union west of the Pripet Marshes.

Then there is the movement for European unity. A great many of us feel the idea is so alien to our outlook that we are inclined to dismiss the movement as visionary and impracticable. But this is beside the point. The point is that nowadays the idea comes quite naturally to millions of people on the Continent. For in Europe the two world wars have been civil wars, tearing the fabric of life to pieces. The fact that they arose out of national quarrels and ambitions is an added reason why reasonable men are unable to stake their hopes for the future on the existing pattern of European society. They pin their hopes on the idea that a larger unity including their country with those of their neighbours might give a more enduring and better framework for life.

I first met the idea in the summer of 1947 when I worked in Paris on the Committee for European Economic Cooperation which framed an answer to General Marshall's offer of help. I still think that conference remarkable because I believe almost every national delegation came to feel a curiously vivid unity of purpose with the others, in spite of the diversity of national needs and national problems. We felt we were doing very much more than draw up a joint shopping list to present to the Americans. We were exploring the structure and needs of a historic society to which we belonged. We were trying, fortified by the prospect of help, to give that society a future. In the words of the French we were trying '*faire l'Europe*'; we were taking one step in the making of Europe.

This movement towards unity took shape in 1949 with the creation of the Council of Europe. True, the Council is only an advisory body, a place for debate. But it has focused thought and defined the issues. It has brought out in sharp relief two views of European unity. The one view is of Europe unified by the collaboration of sovereign states. This co-operation is mainly economic, and its progenitor and exemplar is the O.E.E.C. It does not raise issues of principle about sovereignty. It is the view which has been attractive to Britain and the Scandinavian countries. The second view is radically different. It is not satisfied with simply working together. European unity requires a pooling of sovereignty, a political act of union.

On the first view we make the best of what is: on the second we try to create something new. It is the second view which offers a positive hope to western Europe. It has been embodied in two proposals, expressions—if I may say so—of the genius of the French people: the Schuman Plan for a Coal and Steel Community and the Pleven Plan for a Defence Community. Of these the first has so far succeeded, the second has failed. I am amazed whenever I contemplate the Schuman Plan. If it were simply an attempt to get rid of restrictions and limitations in the coal and steel industries of the Ruhr, Lorraine and the Saar, it would be a large and bold enterprise. But the essential purpose of the Coal and Steel Community is avowedly political. It is an instalment of political union: a frontal attack on the ancient hostility of France and Germany: a limited but real pooling of sovereignty by six nations in a high authority charged with the creation of one great common market. That is what makes the Schuman Plan the expression of a great hope; it offers a different future.

I do not know what the fortunes of the Community will be. It may break down, weakened by the failure of the E.D.C. It may succeed. It may prove to be only the biggest cartel of them all. I do not wish to prophesy. What I said at the beginning of this lecture did not rest on a guess about the future. It rested on historical fact, the decision made by six Governments and their peoples about national sovereignty, their agreement to pool that part of sovereignty which lay in power over the two basic industries of the modern state. Whether the vision of a new Europe expressed in the Schuman Plan forces reality to correspond, or dims and fails, we have seen a historical new beginning, an alteration in the essential character of the Europe we used to know.

But the European Defence Community failed. Proposed by the French, it was voted down by the French Assembly, after Ministers of the six countries had signed the agreement and four parliaments had ratified it. This does not alter my argument. The surprising thing is not that the E.D.C. failed in the end but that it got as far as it did. It shows how uncertain are the lines of the future in men's minds, how wavering the old-established patterns of thought and action have become.

Indeed, I ought not to hide my opinion that the failure of the E.D.C. was by no means foreordained. The group of French statesmen who made the proposal in 1950 were most successful in winning foreign support. But no national campaign was ever launched to persuade the French people. There were nearly four years between the proposal and the vote of the Assembly. The time was not used. That is why the memory of the past was too strong for the revolutionary design of the future.

Lastly, there is Germany. Since 1949 when the west Germans again began to run their own affairs, they have worked as no other western European people has worked. This sustained outburst of energy has been a major event in western Europe. It has made German recovery an accomplished fact. But this is not all. The west Germans now believe they have a future. In part, the belief is based on the bounding pulse of their own vitality. In part, it is based on the knowledge that western Germany is needed by the Atlantic Powers. The free and independent consent of a German Government is again a necessary element in the balance of world power. That the west Germans have a future is certain: what it will be is still obscure, to themselves and to others. For the present German aspirations are large and vague; the steam generated by their red-hot energy, the smoke which shows that once again the volcano has fire in its entrails.

The British people have been hesitant and divided about Germany. Almost all of us have muttered to ourselves that we have been through this door before, twice in the half-century. Surely the right policy must be to stop German rearmament. It can be debated whether once it might have been. Now the time is past. It is our business to concentrate on a different question where the issues are still open. How can we make our policies effective so that, as the west Germans rearm, their company and the extent of their rearming promote the common peace rather than the common destruction?

This then is how I picture the changing forms of western European life. There is the ever-present consciousness of Europe divided, the decay of nationalism, the strong sense that life is provisional. Against this background three things endued with life and with power of growth stand out. This is the new context in which we have to think out our attitude to European affairs.

My purpose is not to comment on particular policies which the British Government has pursued or might pursue. My aim is at once less and more ambitious. It is to identify the basic requirement of policy which we as citizens should take into account when from time to time the Government has to make decisions about Europe. We cannot maintain our traditional attitude in the changed context. Our aim is no longer to prevent the emergence of any preponderant Power in western Europe. It is to secure the emergence, within the Atlantic community, of a particular Power, based on the unity of western European peoples including France and Germany. I am aware that I am advocating a measure of federation. An instalment of federation already exists in the Coal and Steel Community. I believe it to be in our long-term interest to work for further instalments of political union, limited perhaps but real, in western Europe.

What is the justification for the change? We are opposed

to the domination of western Europe by the Soviet Union. We have joined with our friends in the Atlantic Pact to prevent it. Why should we favour the predominance of any other Power? Why break with tradition? There are two other sources from which an attempt to dominate western Europe might spring. Both are real possibilities: a Germany satisfying its supra-national aspirations in an expanding Reich, and the Communist parties of western Europe. Our interest is to prevent both. But by what means? Both Germany and these Communist parties are already in western Europe. We cannot, as in the case of the Soviet Union, join a defensive alliance to prevent their entry. Further, the Germans now believe in a future for Germany; the Communists have faith in the coming of Communist society. The only way to modify or expel positive beliefs is by the force of another positive belief. It takes an idea to deal with an idea. But the only other positive idea in western Europe, the only other movement of thought which has power, is that of the unity of Europe. It already has had a political impact and altered the trend of events. It can take many forms but one element is constant, the positive reconciliation of Germany and France. Without that there is nothing.

It may be asked whether all this is necessary. The Communist parties in western Europe have not gained power in recent years: they have lost power. Western Germany has made an astounding recovery, but the Germans are moving into the Atlantic Community. On inspection the fears dwindle: why go to such lengths to deal with them? But could Britain afford not to take a positive position? I do not think so. For the objection really presupposes that left to themselves things in western Europe would go on much as they are. If the picture I have drawn is at all correct, they certainly will not.

But suppose our neighbours in western Europe were united in this way, would not Britain be overshadowed? Not, I think, in the world of today, where our relations within the Commonwealth and with the United States offset and balance our relationship with western Europe. Politically and economically, we stand to gain, not lose, by having a strong and a prosperous neighbour across the Channel.

If this is the basic requirement of policy, there is something else about which we have to be clear. We shall not be effective if we urge western Europe to act and make no contribution ourselves. It is inadequate just to stand on the touch-line and cheer.

This is a difficult question. I do not think it can be decided by generalities. For example, our friends in western Europe, particularly the French, are apt to urge us to come into full partnership with them. Some Americans take the same line. It is pointed out that the safety of Britain depends on the security of western Europe. Given that there is a risk that Germany might again become a threat, the risk is equal for Britain and France. The answer must be that the policy we commend to France we should practise ourselves. Or again, some of us often say that the other nations of the Commonwealth do not wish Britain to become too deeply committed in Europe. It might cut the Commonwealth ties. I am not contented with either of these answers. The position of Britain in the world is not the same as that of the continental countries of western Europe. And I have rarely, if ever, met Ministers or officials of Commonwealth countries who objected to British commitments in Europe.

No, I think we must look at the facts. What would be involved if political unity in western Europe reached the stage of federal union? At least this much, I think. When I lived in Washington I used occasionally to sit for a few minutes in Lafayette Square, looking across Pennsylvania Avenue at the White House. To the right of the White House I saw the old State Building which used to house the American Foreign Office, and earlier, the Army and Navy Departments as well. To the left, making up the symmetry of the picture, I saw the United States Treasury.

I think I was looking at the essential equipment of a Federal State—an executive, conducting foreign affairs and the defence of the Union, and at the same time controlling the currency and monetary policy, with the power to tax.

If we ask ourselves what we think about this picture, two things I suggest are clear. The first is that as a people we have not got that active sense of belonging to western Europe which would give a political basis for entering on a federal union with our friends. We feel we belong to the British Commonwealth, the other nations of which have joined in with us immediately, twice in this century, when we have had to go to war. The second point is this, and it is equally a fact. We are not prepared to let anyone but ourselves settle our social policies, our policies about employment; and in the modern state these policies are inevitably involved by the control of the currency, monetary policy and the power to tax. It follows from these facts about our state of mind that we are not in a condition to enter a European federation. But there is something else. We often talk of national sovereignty as if it were something precise, indivisible and definite, something we possess or agree to surrender. This does not fit the way the world works today. We and other nations too are at once independent and dependent. This is the practical significance of our association with our friends in the same scale of the world balance of power. It is how the Atlantic Community and N.A.T.O. operate. We have recognised this in our relations with western Europe, in the North Atlantic Treaty, in the original Brussels Pact and in the new Western European Union. Our life and security are not independent of western Europe: they cannot be decided separately from the fate of western Europe. We are positively involved together. Together we sink or swim.

Our attitude to western Europe should be based on this hard fact. We should look round in our empirical fashion for ways of giving effect to it. I think it means neither joining a political union nor rejecting it, but taking out what I shall call a country membership. We pay our subscription and take on our obligations, but not the full subscription nor all the obligations of the regular members, our continental neighbours. It seems to me that recognition of our positive involvement, and giving real effect to it in something this way, was responsible for the great success of the negotiations for a Western European Union.

I should like to feel sure that our thoughts were equally positive about the Coal and Steel Community. Up to the present we have stood aloof and maintained relations with it through a mission as though it were a foreign Power. In my opinion it would be to our advantage if we made an agreement for country membership. We are in a good position, for our steel industry is efficient and highly competitive. And when one looks ahead, we are in fact positively involved by many aspects of the work of the Community: markets, plans for capital investment, wise policies in boom or slump.

We have seen how Britain by taking a positive not a negative attitude, by recognising the plain facts of her positive involvement in the life and security of her neighbours, has taken her place as a leader in western Europe. This was our place at the end of the war. It has not always been so since. Yet it is the place we ought to occupy. If we continue to do so, we shall find that, far from weakening, it reinforces our position in the world.

V

POLITICAL AIMS AND ECONOMIC
STRENGTH

YOU remember our troubles in 1947, 1949, and 1951—the economic crises. I watched them all from abroad. Of one thing I have no doubt: the influence of Britain in the counsels of the nations rose and fell with the strength or weakness of the economy. If one could have drawn a graph of Britain's prestige since the second world war, it would have shown a deep dip in each year of crisis. If these crises had gone on, one every two years, we should soon have found that our friends were ceasing to regard Britain as a Great Power.

So far in these lectures I have been dealing with the changed context of Britain's political relationships and the need to be effective in them. Now I want to take a look at our economic affairs, particularly our dealings with other countries. I do not really think of this as a separate discussion. It is more like the other side of the same penny. When I was a child, before the first world war, there was no problem. The Foreign Office could take the wealth and power of Britain for granted. Today is different.

Moreover it is the context in which we think out economic policies for Britain that makes all the difference. It is easy in this changed world to get the context wrong and make mistakes. I speak with some assurance on this point because eight years ago I made a mistake for precisely this reason. I was composing another set of lectures and drew on my experience at the Ministry of Supply during and just after the war. Perhaps because of the limitations of this experience, I discussed the economic difficulties of Britain in isolation from her enduring associations. This led me to suppose it inevitable that restrictions on our imports and exports would go on for years. Now, when I look back on what I said, I conclude that foreign travel has broadened my mind. I have learned that we cannot secure the future for Britain which we expect, if we accept the inevitability of restrictions on our trade overseas. That is the way to Little England, not to our continuing as a Great Power.

In essentials the right economic context is the same as the political with its three great dimensions. When we realise this, the phrases we hear so often that we get bored by them take on new life. The future of the Sterling Area, the dollar shortage, these name great issues in the real context of our economic affairs. We, as a nation, have to take positions on them.

For the United Kingdom sustains a great role in the world with less to sustain her than any other Great Power. This is the force of what we are told so frequently. Even today we grow only a little more than half our food. We have few raw materials. If we had only our natural resources we could neither work nor live, let alone maintain the standards of the Welfare State; still less could we support the commitments of a Great Power. We have to live, therefore, by the exchanges of foreign trade. To others perhaps imports and exports are just a desirable margin in the business of getting a living; to us they are the means of life. In the City of Bristol there is a society with a great history, the Society of Merchant Venturers. That is what the people of Britain are.

I do not think we always remember this. In recent years a great deal of our interest has been claimed by domestic problems, the redistribution of wealth and insurance against the changes and chances of life. These are problems of distributive justice. They are very important. But when we divide the national resources according to the set of views which prevails, when we distribute claims on future resources, our actions do not directly add anything at all to our wealth or give any guarantee that there will be something to distribute in the future. All the social services, which count for so much in the life of the community, cannot insure or protect us in any way from the risks of a trader's life.

All traders or merchant venturers must cast up their balance at intervals to know where they are. I wonder how many of you look at the figures of the gold and dollar reserves which are published every month in the newspapers. They record the progress of the balance of payments. But what they record is not Britain's balance of payments: it is the Sterling Area's. Of that area, Britain is only a part, though a very important one.

This is a paradox, a paradox which illustrates my thesis. It means that the outcome of the transactions of the whole Sterling Area with the rest of the world is so important to Britain that the Treasury gives us the resulting figures month by month. The unit of thought in terms of which we are invited to consider the external economic affairs of Britain is not Britain by herself but Britain-in-the-Sterling-Area. You know why this is so. It is because our money, the pound sterling, is so much more than Britain's domestic currency. It is the money in which the other countries of the Commonwealth and the British Colonies conduct their foreign trade and keep their reserves. This needs an exception and an addition. Canada is outside the Sterling Area and Eire is a member of it. Otherwise the Sterling Area is by and large the reflection of the British Commonwealth in economic affairs.

In world trade on the whole goods pay for goods. But trade never balances exactly. There are differences to be settled. When the difference in their trade with the rest of the world is against them, the countries of the Sterling Area generally have to settle in cash—gold or dollars. Again, when they earn a surplus from other countries, they bank the proceeds, in the end gold or dollars, with us against payment in sterling. This is the pooling system of the Sterling Area. There is only one large reserve of gold and dollars. It is kept by the Bank of England and is the reserve not only for Britain but for all the other members of the area. This is why the monthly figures are so important for Britain. Obviously we can get into difficulties not only when we have a deficit on our own balance of payments but when the other members of the area have deficits on theirs. The same reserves in the Bank of England take the strain. For us to act as central banker to the Sterling Area can add to the risks we run.

I have heard it argued that it would be best for Britain if the Sterling Area came to an end and the pound sterling ceased to be a great international currency. Then we should be less exposed to misfortunes whose origin and course we cannot control. I disagree with this view. The basic condition of the continuing greatness of Britain is a vigorous Commonwealth. Our first interest is to support it and not to take away its supports. The Sterling Area is the economic aspect of political association. Take it away and the association would be the less. And the exceptional position of Canada does not alter this truth. One of the strong links between the Nations of the Commonwealth is that by and large the movement of goods and money has not been restricted in a world full of such restrictions.

This is a political argument. There are economic reasons as well. If we are to maintain the style of living to which we are accustomed, if we are to play the part in the world which we assume, we need great markets overseas. But the Sterling Area is a great market for us, and it is a natural market, for the other members have economies still in many ways complementary to our own. We send nearly half of all our exports to it. To keep this market we have to be right on the price and quality of the goods we offer. But we start with advantages. For example, there is an obvious advantage in the close business relations which have been built up over generations. There is an advantage in the absence of difficulties about payment and exchange variations. And there is a very real advantage in the easy movement of capital because in fact trade follows loans,

When all is said, our highly industrialised island is only one half of a reality. We are geared to produce so many more manufactures than we can consume. We become whole, we are a living reality, only in relation to the markets we supply. Here in the Sterling Area is a great market already largely ours. It is the first context of our economic life and power.

I know that I have not quite answered the argument about those additional risks. What about the risks of Britain as central banker to the area? They are real. But they can be increased or diminished by the policies we pursue. We are in fact engaged in diminishing them. This has been a principal aim of the recent Commonwealth Economic Conferences and, to judge by the last two years, a successful one. But the main point is this. I am sure that if the Sterling Area had not existed since the war, our Commonwealth partners would have bought much less from us. Our trade would have contracted. But what we need is expansion of exports. So I come back to the paradox of the monthly figures of the reserves. Like all good paradoxes, it rests on sheer common sense. It points up the fact that Britain by herself is an economic abstraction or a starving reality.

I want to draw attention to another feature of these same figures. The movements of the reserves are stated in dollars. Each month the Treasury tells us how many millions of dollars the Sterling Area has gained or lost. Why dollars? The answer is that the central reserves in the Bank of England consist of gold and dollars. Gold is acceptable across the exchanges anywhere in the world. The dollar is the only international currency which is freely convertible with gold and equally acceptable. That is why the monthly figures are given in dollars. They are good anywhere. Since the war Britain and the Sterling Area have been short of dollars, at times critically short. And we have not been alone in this. Nearly every country in the world has had the same troubles. Other troubles, we are told, when shared

5

are halved. The troubles of dollar shortage shared are doubled.

In all this, of course, I am over-simplifying. The Dollar Area is wider than the United States. For instance there is Canada. But all the same it is not wrong to treat the dollar shortage as first and foremost a problem of economic relations with the United States. Here is our central economic problem, how to live in the same world with the United States and at the same time win a prosperous and stable livelihood from it. Just as I believe that the future of the Commonwealth and our political relations with the United States are not separate issues but essentially interdependent, so I am sure that the long-term future of the Sterling Area depends on how we handle the problems of dollar shortage with the United States.

Let me explain what I mean. When I feel depressed about the future of the British economy, which does not often happen, the same picture always comes into my mind. I seem to see a new pattern of the flow of international trade. It by-passes us, leaving Britain in a backwater. I mention this picture, not because it portrays the future, but because it is an extravagant exaggeration of one trend in the world economy. This trend goes back a long way, perhaps to the middle of the nineteenth century. It was about then that some of the colonial areas of the world began to develop their own industries, faster and faster as the decades passed, with two world wars each providing an extra stimulus.

This has meant that the old text-book pattern of complementary trade between the colonial producer of raw materials and foodstuffs and the industrialised mother country has kept on altering. In most cases the old pattern is still there, interlaced with competition between the growing industries of the younger countries and the established industries of the old. But the leading instance and the extreme case of the trend is the United States. It began as a typical colonial economy; now it is by far the greatest industrial power in the world. It has the kind of self-sufficiency one would expect of a continent. There is a great wealth of natural resources, a large population increasing by about 3,000,000 a year, and consequently a gigantic domestic market constantly expanding. And then there is the high and increasing productivity of American industry.

Change of phase in this giant economy can have startling effects on the world outside. For example, the outbreak of war in Korea led the Americans to embark on a major rearmament programme. We did the same. But the scale of the American effort was so great that their demand for imported raw materials and the pace at which they bought sent world prices rocketing upwards. This was the chief cause of one of our crises, the crisis of 1951. Though the Americans produced most of the raw materials they needed at home, they still imported more than anyone else and were the dominant influence on world prices. Besides they are great exporters of manufactures. In my belief, even after allowing for the competition of western Germany, our great competitor is the United States. Here is the full realisation of the trend and here is the germ of truth in my imaginings. This is why the central problem of Britain in economic affairs is to live in the same world with the Americans.

How should we handle this problem? A nation of traders, which are the best risks for us? Must we accept shortage of dollars as permanent or should we set ourselves to overcome it? Some people think we should just be negative. We should decide in principle not to aim at the free movement of trade and payments. Since the war we have had to discriminate against dollar trade. The reasons which have made this necessary will not alter. They lie in the sheer size and power of the American economy. We cannot live with it. In fact, the argument runs, the system which has come about is the right one. There is a Sterling Area and a Dollar Area. Within each trade and payments move freely. The two worlds can coexist if trade between them is carefully controlled. But we must never allow ourselves to be exposed to American competition without protection. And further they say: look at the high productivity of the American economy. The relation between American productivity and our own is not static but dynamic: it changes to our disadvantage.

I doubt it. I doubt whether the adjustments we have to make to keep the advantages of our mutual trade need be so painful. And in any case surely Britain has steadily become more able, not less able, to compete with the United States as the years have gone by since the war. I think too of the results Sir Donald MacDougall obtained when he looked into the evidence for the faster rate of growth of American productivity. He says that while total output per man-hour probably does increase faster in the United States than elsewhere, the difference may not be nearly as great as is sometimes supposed. This sounds to me like a difficulty we can deal with rather than an insuperable obstacle.

We must have economic aims which do not conflict with our political objectives, even frustrate them. And that is exactly what a policy based on the permanence of the dollar gap would do. It would prevent an effective partnership with the United States. You cannot in the long run maintain close political co-operation if you are all the while fighting a series of disengaging manoeuvres on the economic front with discriminatory controls.

It has been one thing to do this as a temporary measure while the British economy is getting back its strength. It would be another to change the aim of British policy. This is what would be involved. For the policy of the British Government in the post-war period has been to relax controls over the movement of trade and payments as fast as was reasonably safe until the pound could again look the dollar full in the face. To reverse this policy must bring our political and economic aims into collision.

Again, it would loosen the ties of the Commonwealth. Look at Canada. If we decided permanently to discriminate

against dollar trade, she would be on the wrong side of the
fence. One thing reacts on another, and I am sure it would
make Canada's position in the Commonwealth progressively
more uncomfortable. And what about South Africa, the
gold producer, already a rather half-and-half member of
the Sterling Area? What would Australia do, faced with
the permanent prospect of discrimination against the United
States and Canada—Australia, already conscious of danger
in the Pacific, and her need to draw closer to the United
States?

I go further. If our political associations were weakened
in this way, our whole economic prospect would be impaired.
There would be a diminished desire to trade with Britain
and a tendency to drive harder bargains. We should move
closer to the picture I see in rare moments of depression,
the picture of Britain in a backwater. For our external
relations, political and economic, are one whole.

Perhaps you may feel that I am making rather heavy
weather about all this. Think of what has been done in the
last two or three years to reduce discrimination against the
dollar and make trade and payments freer. Think too of
the increase in the central reserves over the period. Why
go on arguing, you may say? We are almost there. We
have made great progress, certainly. And I agree about the
increase in the reserves. But there are still some stages of
the journey to travel.

Our reserves, whilst much better, are still not very big
—about $3,000 millions. The 1951 crisis cost us over
$2,000 millions before we could stop the flow. We had a
good year in 1953, Britain and the Sterling Area. We
added nearly $700 millions to the central reserves. But of
these $500 millions were special receipts by Britain—de-
fence aid, money spent here by Canadian and American
troops and the like. In the rest of the Sterling Area the
good surplus earned by the Colonies hid a deficit of nearly
$100 millions from the other member countries. Certainly
it was a good year, but there were some weaknesses as well

as strength. Besides the dollar shortage is not over in the rest of the world. It has been masked in various ways, but there is still an underlying dollar gap of some billions. This is important, for if we and the Sterling Area stopped discriminating against the dollar, we might find that other countries, for example in western Europe, might prefer to use the sterling they earned to buy dollars from us rather than British goods. The fact that they were still hungry for dollars would increase the pressure on us.

When the Chancellor of the Exchequer was in Washington last September he described British policy as 'a collective approach to freer trade and payments'. This reminded me of something I learned in the war. I learned that the greatest problems were most successfully met by doing something of everything that helped towards a solution rather than by exclusive reliance on one or two remedies. The Americans can help us. The dollar shortage is not all of our making: they have contributed to it themselves. They still do not behave as one might reasonably expect of the world's greatest creditor nation. 'If you want us to reduce discrimination', the Chancellor of the Exchequer said to them, 'the answer is to reduce it yourselves'. Indeed, we want help from all our friends. But in the last resort what we do is decisive. Our friends will be helpful if they believe in us and our policies. The root of the matter is in us.

In a way, the British economy is like a watch. If its performance is to be satisfactory, the hairspring and the mainspring must both be in order, the regulator and the prime mover. If the hairspring is not, breakfast may be signalled at tea-time and utter confusion prevail. But if the mainspring is not working, there is nothing even to go wrong. In the British economy the hairspring consists of those regulatory devices, fiscal and monetary measures, which help to keep the economy in trim and free from the disturbances of inflation. They can do a great deal, and to our great benefit, provided they are not asked to do too much. They cannot substitute for the mainspring of the economy.

What is this? It is our power to produce, to be flexible and efficient in production. If all this is strong, the economy moves forward and gains in strength. The strength, it is true, can be dissipated if we do not regulate ourselves wisely. If we give way to inflation, as we have known only too well since the war, costs go up, we become less competitive, we consume too much at home. But our life and strength as a nation of traders, earning a living overseas, turns on our power to produce and our efficiency at the job.

In the end we face a moral issue. Everything turns on what we are willing to do. Remember this about the future we assume for Britain. A wise foreign policy will improve our prospects: lack of statesmanship could ruin them. But our prospects ultimately depend on the performance of the economy. There lie the means of greatness.

VI

THE ISSUE BEFORE US

WE have to make a choice in the next ten, perhaps in the next fifteen, years. We can live half in a dream and behave as if the world had not changed greatly or our position in it. We can live as if we need not bestir ourselves; as if the British Commonwealth was sure to go on of its own accord; as if it did not matter whether we get the Americans wrong or they misunderstand us; as if Europe was still the Europe we used to know; as if we could ignore the direct connection between the effort we make at home, our flexibility and efficiency in production, and our prospects in the world. Or we can live wide-awake to the changes round us and take our opportunity. We can be leaders and have a position out of all proportion to our population or our physical resources. We can make a real contribution to settling the great problems of the world.

I have said little about these problems: the divison between the Communist bloc and the rest of us, the new nationalism of Asia, the steady increase of armaments, atomic and hydrogen bombs. I have left them out on purpose. I am sure we can brood too much on the Iron Curtain and the metaphysics of coexistence, on the possibilities of a third world war and mass destruction. We can be so fascinated by the dangers we contemplate that we lose the power to act. Sudden and uncontrollable catastrophe is possible, but it is no good looking at the future simply in terms of that hypothesis. The probability is that these problems and dangers are all long-term. We are going to go on living with them. There are no quick answers. I think it is obvious that we have a contribution to make. We have a sense of history. We know how to combine resolution in purpose with moderation in action. We are accustomed to making time an ally, but not an excuse. We might make the difference between peace and war.

We therefore face a moral issue. By our choice we shall declare what sort of people we are. My reading of history is that the British people have always been prepared to undertake and carry through what they believed necessary for the continuing greatness of their country. They have shown this in time of war and they have shown it again in these years of troubled peace. But their readiness always depends on a condition. It is this. They must see clearly and be convinced that what is said to be necessary really is so. How are we to reach conviction and stop being in danger of gently deceiving ourselves, pretending that we do not really face such a choice or hoping that what we should like will happen anyhow, without our having to bother?

I said that the choice we make will show what sort of people we are. I had something precise in mind. In this half-century we have been forced to see that we cannot take civilisation or freedom for granted. A free society is a great achievement. But it is also a difficult thing, and fragile. To keep it, you have to work away at it all the time. Our kind of free society is a total democracy. By our choice we shall show whether we can carry its responsibilities or whether it is going to be too difficult for us. Here we confront yet another of our problems, the change we have made in ourselves. For total democracy is a new thing. In the United Kingdom it is the child of the twentieth century. To my mind it is still in the experimental stage.

Total democracy is democracy carried to its limit. In the United Kingdom it means that all men and women of twenty-one years of age and over have the vote. It has been natural, and perhaps inevitable, that the first effect of all having the vote has been to focus interest on the distribution of wealth. It has increasingly become the centre of controversy between the political parties. It has led to nonsense about the problems of production being solved while those of distribution were still to be worked out. The general effect has been to emphasise political division. And this has been further stressed by the power of the great party machines developed to get the mass vote out, the narrow margins of victory at general elections, the importance attached to party loyalty.

This emphasis is a weakness, for our kind of political democracy depends as much on the recognition of unity as on the fact of division. The recognition of a common responsibility for the interests of the whole community, the acknowledgement that here are national issues which should be debated and settled outside of party, the self-discipline in controversy entailed by these beliefs—these maintain the unity of a free society which alone makes party disputes healthy and constructive. They are our safeguard against civil strife, against the emergence of force as the arbiter of disputes.

I feel sure that if I were regularly present when the House of Commons is sitting, I should often feel that the quality of the debate was near that of a Council of State, with party advantage forgotten for the moment. But I am not—like nearly all of us. From the outside I catch more easily and more regularly the echo of disciplined feet marching into the lobbies, division after division.

On the great questions of national importance which are outside party, we, the mass electorate, do not hear enough from our leaders. We need to be better informed, on foreign affairs, on economic matters, about what falls within our common responsibility for the general interest. How else can we give that measure of intelligent support to the Government without which democracy grows weak?

There is a risk of too wide a gap developing between those who govern us and us who are governed. The gap grows naturally; it is closing it which takes thought and effort. We have to spend most of our time looking after our own affairs and taking an interest in the churches, groups or clubs to which we belong. It is not easy to rise suddenly to a national point of view and look at the problems of Britain, overseas and at home, as responsible citizens. But those who govern us spend their working days on these problems. Their job is to take account of the changed world in which we live. They are accustomed to the complexities of our relations with our friends. Their outlook, their approach to the problems, the methods they use, differ from our habits of thought.

It is at this point that some people take refuge in the notion of strong leadership. I should be the last to deny the need for the Government to lead or its duty to do so. But the mystique of leadership does not fit in with our kind of democracy. Nothing can take the responsibilities of the citizens from them. Surely in Britain leadership is a complex and delicate art, and successful leadership depends as much on the enlightened support of the led as on the inspiration of the leader. If therefore we are to narrow the gap between those who govern us and ourselves, we shall need help from our leaders and we shall also have to help ourselves. But as we succeed and prove we can carry our responsibilities, we shall at the same time see more clearly and, I believe, choose rightly about the future of Britain. The moral issue with which I began and the operation of total democracy come together. Our governments will be able to carry through the broad policies we must adopt only if we understand and support them.

I shall be told that this is not realistic. If seeing clearly and choosing rightly about the broad future of Britain is to be the function of the general body of voters, then it will never happen. It implies an idealised, a perfectionist view of human nature. And if you expect too much from human beings, you end by getting nothing. It is no good making everything depend on the response of the many. I disagree. And this is the heart of the matter. Our political tradition is built on the ability and willingness of the voting citizen to be interested in the general questions of the community and take some individual responsibility for their solution.

We presuppose a sufficient degree of unity and common purpose to be able to settle our affairs in debate. We have faith in reason as the chief weapon of democracy, not believing for one moment that we are purely rational beings but holding that reason can regulate our other activities and prevent a resort to force.

These are built-in presuppositions of British society. They were at work in the decision to make education universal in 1870. They helped to lay the foundations of a general secondary education in 1902. We were sure that the spark of reason was alive in everyone and could be brought out and developed. Total democracy is the test of our political faith. It is far harder to get understanding of the broad problems of the nation widely spread through the mass electorate than it was with the minority electorates of the last century. True, but this is the only direction of advance. It is implied by all we have done. After all the price of keeping our free society is more than eternal vigilance: it is going on working at it.

I want to illustrate the sort of thing we can do. There are fields where I think we must first be helped by our rulers; there are others where we can do a good deal to help ourselves. As an example of the first, I take foreign affairs, both political and economic. We should gain a good deal if our leaders were rather less cautious in approaching the whole body of citizens, if they were more experimentally minded. This is the age of radio and television. And the old tag is true: seeing is believing. The power of television is great and will be used. They could put it to good use. What I observed in the United States makes me sure of this, as it also impressed on me the importance of mastering these new techniques of mass communication with the citizens in their homes.

If our leaders would stimulate general discussion in the nation more often, outside the lines of party, on some of the broad attitudes we should adopt to the changed world, the nation would be more effective. And later, when they

came to particular decisions, they would enjoy stronger
and more understanding support and run less risk that sudden popular emotion would frustrate their efforts. Experiments like this would not infringe on the rights and privi-
leges of Parliament. What the citizen needs is to be helped
to think out the general background of policy, the long-
term assessments of the situation which lie behind the
actual conduct of affairs.

There are difficulties. One springs from the progress of
general education in Britain over the last eighty years. For
education both builds and destroys. It is destructive of
established authority and traditional opinion. The authority
it recognises and respects is that of experience, of the man on
the job, the man with active responsibility. These have the
right to be heard and believed. In our political system
Ministers of the Crown and their advisers, members of the
Foreign and the Civil Service, alone in their different ways
have the authority of direct experience. They are the people
who are on the job.

The Ministers of the Crown most closely concerned with
these matters in any Government are the Foreign Secretary
and the Chancellor of the Exchequer. I have worked with
more than one Foreign Secretary and more than one Chancellor of the Exchequer. I know how hard driven they
are. There is little time or energy to spare after the proper
demands of Parliament, of their departments, and of conferences overseas. They can hardly add to their duties. The
question—and it is a big question—is whether the priorities
are right. I am suggesting the case for revision.

Then there are Foreign Servants and Civil Servants. It
is our pride that the public service is outside party politics
and serves whichever party is in power. But members of the
Foreign Service, when posted abroad, frequently find themselves making speeches and leading discussions on foreign
affairs. And at home I have noticed in recent years that
senior members of the Civil Service have had rather more
freedom to talk in public on the background of their work.

I suggest that, if a wider knowledge of the background and general direction of foreign policy is urgently required among us all, there is room for a variety of experiments in closing the gap between us and them. This need not conflict with any essential principle. For myself, I am more worried by the risks of trying to guide twentieth-century democracy by nineteenth-century methods.

I was interested, when in the United States, to watch an experiment the State Department was making. In 1951, for instance, officials of the Department went out into the forty-eight States of the Union and made nearly 2,500 speeches. Meetings were held in the State Department, at the rate of one a week, to explain to various groups and organisations the broad aims of American policy. Beyond that there were regional conferences at which the heads of national organisations discussed foreign policy with members of the Department. I know that one can never success-fully transplant an American practice into the British scene, any more than one can do the reverse. But the problems of the mass electorate face the Americans in their continent as they face us in our islands. We can afford to view such experiments with indifference only when we know we have better answers ourselves.

My second example comes from the field of economic affairs. Our Governments since the war have repeatedly appealed to us for restraint about wages and wisdom in the use of profits. I must admit that for a time I thought this advice sensible rather than profound. But now I believe the point to be of a different order. Our Governments, it seems to me, have become aware of a new working principle in our democracy. They have insisted on it because, unless we see it too and act accordingly, our free society is endangered. But to think through and apply a new working principle in the life of the community is a major matter. It continues to be the business of us all because it is a question of our general attitude to life and work.

Let me explain what I am driving at. You know how

the political parties are agreed that the state should aim at maintaining a high and stable level of employment. You know, too, that experience since the war suggests this aim can be achieved. High employment and the steady growth of production have enabled us to make great advances. These advances have brought other things with them. Almost anyone can find work. Profits are good, because demand is kept high enough to absorb what is produced. Again, labour shortage and good profits together reduce resistance to wage increases.

Wage increases which come from greater efficiency of production are very good things. But when they do not, and the increase is passed on in higher prices, it does little good to those who get more and harm to those who do not. What is more, if this happens regularly, it whittles away the value of money. And if inflation gets out of hand, the danger is great. The line of argument is familiar, but the dangers are real. It is not an accident that there is a general round of wage increases nearly every year, nor that the cost of living has more or less kept pace with the movement of wage rates. With steady high employment, both employers and workers may become less conscious of the need for efficiency. A nation of manufacturers and traders, we may not increase our efficiency fast enough to compete and win in world markets.

How do we keep the great advantage of high employment and avoid these dangers? It is here that the new working principle comes in. To succeed we have to practise what our Governments preach: cultivate restraint and exert a real self-discipline. It is not something we can do once for all; as with the other requisites of freedom we have to keep on at it all the time. After all the agreed policy of high employment goes a long way to guarantee the interests of both employers and workers. It is no longer enough for them simply to drive hard bargains with each other: they have their common responsibility for the public interest. Where restrictive practices exist on either side of industry, developed in the days when unemployment was widespread and competition really cut-throat, it is time for them to go.

This issue I am discussing cannot arise in a communist country. If managers are not efficient or workers do not work, they disappear into concentration camps. In a free country with heavy unemployment, the hard discipline of the competitive struggle keeps everyone up to the mark. In our free society, our total democracy, we have chosen freedom both from the compulsion of the state and from the compulsion of want. But the law of the survival of the fittest is always there. We can survive and succeed only if we substitute something positive, the intelligent self-discipline of free men. This is difficult. The democracy we practise is a difficult and demanding way of life. But what is at stake is the future of our society, and at the same time our willingness to grasp our opportunity and be effective in the world.

One of the things which struck my imagination when I lived in the United States was the American attitude to efficient production and technological advance. Americans were fascinated by the scientific technique of continuous discovery. They regarded an idea as old, a technological advance as obsolete, a new product as obsolescent, the very moment the idea had been exploited, the improvement carried out, the product made. This is one of the secrets of the American way of life. They feel that perpetual innovation, this ever-repeated assertion of man's power over nature, has an absolute value. They know that in the expanding economy of the United States these activities have paced the development of their country and transformed their standard of living. But there is more to it than that. These activities are a triumphant assertion of the spirit of man.

Most of us do not feel like this. Our traditions are different. We recognise the high place of pure science. For centuries men have found enduring satisfaction in exploring the mysteries of nature. But applied science, engineering, the process of industry—no, these are not on the same footing. Most useful, no doubt, but not inherently distinguished. Indeed we are apt to think that most of the valuable things in life are outside the factory or office. Men really live in their leisure. Work has a subordinate excellence. It should be done well because it is necessary.

Perhaps, but we have to live in the same world with the Americans and compete with them. We have to find an extra bit of purpose and zest over and above the regular motives of daily life. Most people work better if they believe that what they do matters and makes a contribution to their community. If we saw clearly how directly the greatness of Britain depends on our productive efficiency, we should find that extra bit of drive. For making our industries adaptable and flexible is not just the problem of employers and workers. We are all of us involved for in the end success or failure flows from the climate of opinion, the scale of values of us all.

Take one example. Think of the problem of power, a large part of productive efficiency. Our workers have at their elbow about one third of the power at the disposal of American workers. We must have more, and it cannot all come from coal. This means developing the industrial uses of nuclear energy and pressing forward fast. And we are well placed. Britain has more than her share of inventive genius; we have a start of ten years over most other countries, except the United States and Russia; and we have an industry big enough to tackle the job. The programme calls for a large and increasing diversion of resources from the immediate comfort and convenience of living. Are we, the voting citizens, ready to choose and forgo what we would like now to make sure of the future of Britain?

Or take another illustration, just one of many—the question of working two day shifts. This is becoming increasingly important in sections of the engineering industry. In order to compete, firms find they must instal more complex and costly machinery. But often, if our prices are to be competitive with American prices, the new equipment must be used for more than eight hours a day. You might think this was essentially a specialised matter for industry, for managements and workers. I think not. It is just as much the problem of the whole community. You can see that this must be so. For the different times of starting and stopping work with two shifts a day mean alterations in the whole framework of life. Buses and trains have to run at different times. Shops and restaurants have to alter their hours. Radio and television, the other interests of leisure, have to change their programmes. So it is our problem too. Are we willing to put ourselves about for the sake of efficiency in industry? We have to choose.

When I began this lecture, I spoke of the opportunity of Britain and the contribution we might make to the settlement of the great problems of the world. I have just been talking of working two shifts a day, shopping hours and bus timetables. I think you may feel this an anticlimax.

But is it? It follows the pattern of life. No vision was ever realised except in the humdrum daily round. No hopes ever came true except in the life of every day. The choice for Britain must be made and the job carried out in ordinary life and work. In our free society the vision, the choice and the work are for all. None of us can leave it to others. This is the privilege of freedom, and the enduring responsibility we carry. Britain will continue a Great Power; she will be a leader among the nations and take her part in the great decisions; she will have the economic strength to sustain her role—if we make it our daily business. It is there that we become masters of our fate. Action begins in the workaday world, if we will to be great.